THE WORLD'S
══WORST══
PREDICTIONS

Also in Arrow by Graham Nown
ODDBALLS (with Dave Dutton)

THE WORLD'S
WORST
PREDICTIONS

Graham Nown

Illustrated by Albert

ARROW BOOKS

Arrow Books Limited
17–21 Conway Street, London WIP 6JD

An imprint of the Hutchinson Publishing Group

London Melbourne Sydney Auckland
Johannesburg and agencies throughout
the world

First published 1985

© Graham Nown 1985

Illustrations © Albert Ruisling

Set in Linotron Ehrhardt by
Rowland Phototypesetting Limited
Bury St Edmunds, Suffolk

Printed and bound in Great Britain by
Anchor Brendon Limited, Tiptree, Essex

ISBN 0 09 937400 5

CONTENTS

ACKNOWLEDGEMENTS

Grateful thanks for suggestions and contributions to Gabriel Bowman, *Financial Times*; Robin Craig, University College, London; Sir Robin Day; Kieran Devaney, Radio City; Dave Dutton; the *Guardian* library; Don Higgs, *Titbits*; David Hodgkinson, *Daily Star*; John Kelly, *The Economist*; Bill McMillan, Director of Information, UKAEA; Jean Rook; Andrew Rosthorn, *Sunday Mirror*; Jonathan Wootliff, the Letter Writing Bureau

INTRODUCTION

Crystal Balls

Niels Bohr, the Danish physicist born a century ago, got it right. 'Prediction is very difficult,' he concluded, 'especially about the future.'

Ample proof of his wisdom is all around us. Scientists, showbiz stars, sportsmen and politicians have a habit of opening their mouths, then sooner or later wishing they hadn't.

The trait has spawned a whole multi-million pound industry – Public Relations. If people in the public eye didn't make bloomers, half the PR men who pick up the pieces would be out of business. So, come to think of it, would lawyers and newspapermen.

From dukes to dustmen, we are all prone to foot in mouth. The journalist who says he has never made a gaffe must either be sober, or talking to a non-journalist. Duff predictions are an occupational hazard.

Those who labour through the night to share the blunders of others with millions are exuberant connoisseurs of cock-ups perpetrated in their own nest. I hope one or two in this slim volume will swell the collection.

Perhaps we should have all listened to Eugene Ionesco's advice. 'You can predict things only after they've happened,' he said. Then again, he only wrote plays, didn't he?

Graham Nown

7

THERE'S NO BUSINESS . . .

Show Biz and the Arts

'Ah, what is man?' mused music hall star Dan Leno. 'Wherefore does he why? Whence did he whence? Whither is he whithering?'

Whither indeed . . . Clark Gable was told he had ears like taxicab doors, Wagner was asked if he was a human being at all. Even Jesus heard, presumably, that he wasn't as big as the Beatles. But that's show biz.

Stars rise and fall, and in between they flicker a little. 'You'll never find anyone to sing those songs,' Anne Bancroft once told the producers of a new show called 'Funny Girl'.

It's that ring of supreme confidence – like the row which ran into litigation over the first four bars of the 'Hallelujah Chorus' from the *Messiah*. In 1923 Handel's publishers took the writers of 'Yes, We Have No Bananas' to court, accusing them of blatant plagiarism.

Some of the biggest blunders have been in the failure to recognize raw talent: the four record companies who turned down the Beatles, and Sam Phillips of Sun Records who overlooked Elvis. Even Tiny Tim's mother told him he'd never be a star with a squeaky voice like that. He went on to prove her wrong. At least, I think he did.

So next time you see Rita Ramsbottom and her Performing Poodles, don't laugh – they may be in the Cabinet one day.

AN ILL WIND

'Forget it. No civil war picture ever made a nickel.'
Film producer Irving Thalberg on being
offered *Gone with the Wind*, 1938

DAY OF THE JACKASS

'No reader interest . . .'
W. H. Allen, 1970. Publisher's verdict on
rejecting Frederick Forsyth's manuscript
of *The Day of the Jackal*. It sold eight
million copies

THE ALL-SEEING EYE

'Ladies and gentlemen, I shall now drive this car blind-
fold through the centre of Ilford . . .'
Romark the Hypnotist, 1977.
Approximately two minutes later he
collided with a parked police van

YEAH, YEAH, YEAH

'The Beatles? They're on the wane . . .'
Prince Philip, 1965

NEXT, PLEASE – 1

'One day I'll be a star.'
Singer Tony Hill, whose record 'Old King
Cole', with heavy synthesizer backing,
sold one copy

SOMEONE'S HEAD WENT ON THE BLOCK

'Any similarity to actual persons or events is unintentional . . .'

> Disclaimer, hastily removed from 1938
> film credits of *Marie Antoinette*

NUTCRACKER

'. . . that scoundrel Brahms. What a giftless bastard! It annoys me that this self-inflated mediocrity is hailed as genius.'

> Tchaikovsky, 1886

NEXT, PLEASE – 2

'I was knocked out when I heard it. It's going to be a great hit.'

> Singer Tony Hill on his record 'I am a
> Pirate King', from Gilbert and Sullivan's
> *The Pirates of Penzance*. Total sales: eleven
> copies

SILENTS, PLEASE

'Who the hell wants to hear actors talk?'

> Hollywood film mogul Harry Warner,
> 1921

THE KILLER FROM THE KILLER

'I guarantee that if Elvis had his choice of being up in heaven right now, or coming on before me, he'd have to come on before me. There's no way Elvis can follow me.'

> Jerry Lee Lewis, *c.* 1970

'I don't care what people say, I want to be a star. I think I'll make it this time, but the tune is a bit weak . . .'

> Singer Tony Hill, on his record 'The Cuckoo Clock' which went on to sell three copies worldwide

LORD OF THE FLIES

'There is really no one who can appreciate him. He is a little English phenomenon of no special interest . . .'

> Artur Lundkvist of the Nobel Literature panel, assessing William Golding who won the Nobel Prize for literature, 1983

COME IN No. 7, YOUR TIME'S UP

'If this piece is not by some means abridged, it will soon fall into disuse.'

> Boston music critic Philip Hale on Beethoven's Seventh Symphony, 1837

FRANK WHO?

'No commercial potential.'

> Frank Zappa's verdict on the early Mothers of Invention

IN THE PINK

'As long as I live I will never be party to anything as un-American as a blacklist . . .'

> Eric Johnston, president of the US Association of Motion Picture Producers, 1947

'We will not knowingly employ a communist in this industry.'

Press release issued by Eric Johnston,
late 1947

BUT CAN HE JUGGLE?

'Can't act. Can't sing. Slightly bald. Can dance a little.'

Studio report on Fred Astaire's first
screen test, 1932

IT'S GOSPEL

'The Beatles are just a passing phase, symptoms of the uncertainty of the times and the confusion about us.'

Billy Graham, *c.* 1968

NO PESSIMISM, PLEASE

'It'll only run a few weeks . . .'

Antony Marriott, co-writer of 'No Sex
Please We're British', 1971. Almost three
million people have enjoyed the show

RIVER OF NO RETURN

'You'd better learn secretarial work, or else get married.'

Model agent Emmeline Snively to Marilyn
Monroe, 1944

EASTON PROMISE

'The singer will have to go, the BBC won't like him.'

Eric Easton, co-manager of the Rolling
Stones, 1962

GATHERING MOSS

'I give the Stones about another two years. I'm saving for the future. I bank all my song royalties, for a start.'

Mick Jagger, 1964

I'LL DO IT MY WAY

'Rock and roll is sung, written and played for the most part by cretinous goons.'

Frank Sinatra, *c.* 1962

DON'T CALL US

'In my opinion, she's nix.'

Howard Hughes, on seeing Jean Harlow's
first screen test, 1929

WAKEY WAKEY!

'The teenage vogue for beat music and rock and roll is over.'

BBC Press Office, 1960

CASH FLOW CRISIS

'*Das Kapital* will not even pay for the cigars I smoked writing it.'

Karl Marx, 1867, after publication of the
first volume of *Kapital*

GOING DOWN

'Hi ho! Hi ho! It's off to work we go . . .'
The twenty-eight-strong cast of *Snow White and the Seven Dwarfs*, at Moretonhampstead, Devon, 1984, before disappearing in a cloud of dust when the stage collapsed

'Two left in the cellar!'

QUEUE HERE

THEORY OF EVOLUTION

'You care for nothing but shooting, dogs and rat catching. You will be a disgrace to yourself and your family.'
Charles Darwin's father to the young C.D., 1820

SHOOTING HIS BOLT

'Boris Karloff announces he has finished with Franken-stein and will now only accept sympathetic roles.'

> Karloff's press agent, 1947. Boris went on
> to make twenty more horror films,
> including *Frankenstein* (1958)

THEY WERE BIG IN JAPAN, THOUGH

'We don't think that the Beatles will do anything in this market.'

> Jay Livingstone, CBS records, 1964.
> Spoken as the Fab Four were poised to
> take America by storm

NOT TERRIBLY UPLIFTING

'Unphotogenic . . .'

> Fox Studios screen test report on Jane
> Russell, 1940

FRANKLY, MY DEAR . . .

'I wouldn't pay fifty thousand bucks for any damn book any damn time.'

> Hollywood mogul Jack Warner,
> dismissing the exclusive rights to *Gone
> with the Wind*, 1938

HE SOLD ELVIS, TOO

'I knew Roy Orbison's voice was pure gold, but I felt he'd be dead inside a month if people saw him.'

> Sam Phillips, Sun Records, c. 1970

THE WRITING'S ON THE WALL

'Commercially unacceptable . . .'
> AIP verdict on *American Graffiti* when
> invited to contribute financial backing

THE FAB FLOPS

'We don't like the sound – guitar groups are on the way out.'
> Decca A&R man Dick Rowe on being
> offered the Beatles, 1962

OH BOY!

'Dear George – Many thanks for taking the trouble to supply us with material on your band Culture Club. However, after careful consideration, it was our feeling that the group wouldn't be right for the program.'
> David Croft, BBC-TV assistant producer,
> 1980, letter to Boy George

THE DAY JOB

'I want to manage those four boys. It wouldn't take me more than two half days a week.'
> Brian Epstein after meeting the Beatles, 1961

THE LAST WORD

'God is dead.'
> Friedrich Nietzsche, *c.* 1980

'Nietzsche is dead.'
> God

FRANK AND FEARLESS

The World's Press

Newspapers, like politicians, have a knack of ignoring their bloomers. By the next edition they are thundering forth as if nothing had happened.

To be fair, the occasional twinge of conscience does creep in. When the *New York Times*, for instance, lambasted the idea of rocket power, it apologized – forty-nine years later, after the Apollo 11 flight.

Sticking your neck out and trumpeting works fine if you are right, especially on the sports page. But the endearing thing about newspapers is that even gaffes on the level of the 1939 classic 'There Will Be No War' are taken in good humour. A few sackings here, an editorial reshuffle there, and the whole thing's forgotten.

Everyday bloomers would go on the noticeboard if one had been made big enough to take them. Some perhaps will never be surpassed: 'MACARTHUR FLIES BACK TO FRONT', the legendary 'BRITISH PUSH BOTTLES UP GERMANS', or the promising 'MAGISTRATES TO ACT ON INDECENT SHOWS'.

My own favourite for many years was 'MENDELSSOHN CHOIR SWEEPS BUFFALO OFF ITS FEET'. I often wondered if it lived to roam. If we read tomorrow's papers we may find out . . .

ROYAL FLUSH

'Charles to Marry Astrid – Official!'
Daily Express, June 1974

TIN HELMETS ESSENTIAL

'And for the tourist who really wants to get away from it all – safaris in Vietnam.'
Newsweek, 1959, predicting holidays in the 1970s

NO SMOKE WITHOUT FIRE

'Mount Pelee is no more to be feared than Vesuvius is feared by Naples. Where would one be better off than in St Pierre?'

Les Colonies, St Pierre, Lesser Antilles, 1902. Twenty-four hours later Mount Pelee erupted, killing the entire 30,000 population

APART FROM THAT, IT WAS FINE

'It is poison, rank poison. This man Wagner was born to feed spiders with flies, not to make happy the heart of man with beautiful melody and harmony. He is incapable of writing a tune.'

Review of *Lohengrin*, *London Music Journal*, 1855

MAN SPEAK WITH SOUTHFORK TONGUE

'A limited series with a limited future . . .'
Daily Variety, 1978, on the first episode of 'Dallas'

TAKE IT FROM US . . .

'The *Daily Express* Declares That Britain Will Not Be Involved In A European War This Year Or Next Year Either.'

Daily Express, 1938

IT'S A JUNGLE OUT THERE

'Kipling, you just don't know how to use the English language.'

Editor of the *San Francisco Examiner*, firing
Rudyard Kipling in 1869

PARDON ME, YOUR SLIP'S SHOWING

'I understand no other designer has been approached by Buckingham Palace, which makes the choice of Zandra (Rhodes) a mere formality.'

Jean Dobson, *Daily Mail*, 1981, shortly
before it was revealed that the
Emmanuels had been asked to design
Princess Diana's wedding dress

YOU'RE NEVER ALONE WITH AN AD REP

'The trade of advertising is now so near to perfection that it is not easy to propose any improvement.'

The Idler, 1759

RICHARD WHO?

'There will be no west coast interest in this story.'

Charles Thierot, publisher, *San Francisco
Chronicle*, 1974, turning down the rights to
the Watergate story

EAGER BEAVER

'I am convinced that Mr Churchill will carry his party to victory.'

Lord Beaverbrook, weeks before
Churchill lost the 1945 election

NICE TRY, BOYS

'UFOs will buzz Camp David while President Reagan is in weekend retreat, forcing him to announce officially that they exist . . .

'Liz Taylor and Richard Burton will remarry . . .

'Julian Lennon will form a band called the New Beatles, featuring musicians who bear eerie resemblances to Paul McCartney, George Harrison and Ringo Starr . . .

'An Argentinian death squad will try to assassinate Margaret Thatcher, but will fail . . .

'Monaco will be the scene of a spectacular fairy-tale wedding when Prince Albert weds Caroline Kennedy . . .

'Frank Sinatra will have a nervous breakdown and retire to a South Pacific island . . .

'Queen Elizabeth will step down and Prince Charles will take over the throne . . .'

And I will be fired from the National Enquirer.

Predictions for 1983 in the *National Enquirer*, one of America's biggest-selling weekly magazines

KEEP TAKING THE TABLETS

'Better a wise apothecary than a starved poet – so back to the shop, Mr John, back to plasters, pills and ointment boxes.'

Review of Keat's 'Endymion', *Blackwood's*
magazine *c.* 1820

CLASSIC COCK-UP

'Sterility may be inherited.'

Pacific Rural News, *c.* 1965

A QUIET YEAR AHEAD

'In this column for years, I have constantly laboured these points: Hitler's horoscope is not a war horo-scope . . . .'

Astrologer R. H. Naylor, *Sunday Express*,
1939

SOME YOU WIN . . .

'I am reliably informed that the couple are expecting a princess.'

Nigel Dempster, *Daily Mail*, before the
birth of Prince William, 1982

DON'T GET AROUND MUCH ANY MORE

'Bandleaders come and go, but the perennial Duke Ellington, like Tennyson's brook, seems destined to go on forever.'

Bath & West Evening Chronicle, 1974.
Duke Ellington died twenty-four hours later

ROCK OF AGES

'Is this boy TV star too sexy?'
Daily Sketch, 1958, on Cliff Richard
before his vow of chastity

BOLSHIE

'What are the Bolsheviki? They are representatives of the
most democratic government in Europe. . . . Let us recognize the truest democracy in Europe, the truest democracy in the world today.'
American newspaper tycoon, William
Randolph Hearst, 1918

THAT'S THE TROUBLE WITH ARI

'I think we can tell you with comparative assurance that
Aristotle Onassis is not likely to be marrying Jackie
Kennedy, or anyone else.'
Syndicated columnist, Earl Wilson, 1968,
shortly before the marriage was
announced

BETTER LUCK NEXT TIME

'Slater Walker is now safe from calamity.'
Sunday Telegraph, 1975, the year Slater
Walker collapsed

EVERYBODY'S DADA

'. . . without doubt, a benevolent, honest, dedicated and
hardworking man.'
Financial Times, 1972, on Idi Amin

HARPING ON

'The actual building of roads devoted to motor cars is not for the near future, in spite of many rumours to that effect.'

Harper's Weekly, 1902

OIL ON TROUBLED WATERS

At the height of petrol rationing in 1974, the *Economist* boldly ran a leader entitled: 'The Coming Glut of Energy.'

TRIB-ULATION

'Dewey Defeats Truman.'

Chicago Tribune, 1948. First edition headline confidently printed before the presidential election results came through. Truman, of course, won by a landslide

'We carried out an opinion poll on newspapers and we came bottom!'

CHICAGO TRIBUNE

WHERE THERE'S LIFE

'We do not intend to go out of business. We do not foresee going out of business. We have no contingency plans for going out of business.'

> Gary Valk, publisher of *Life* magazine
> 1971. The following year *Life* went out of
> business

VOICE OF THE PEOPLE

'Anything more dull and commonplace, it would not be easy to reproduce . . .'

> *The Times*, 1863, on Abraham Lincoln's
> Gettysburg address

ROOKIE REPORTER

'So long as you live, you will never get to Fleet Street.'

> Hull newspaper editor to Jean Rook

EVER BEEN HAD?

'We are absolutely certain of the authenticity of this biography . . .'

> McGraw-Hill executive Donald M.
> Wilson, 1971, on Clifford Irving's spoof
> biography of Howard Hughes

HE AIN'T NUTHIN' . . .

'Singing in any form is foreign to Elvis.'

> *Daily Mail*, 1956

OUTLOOK UNCERTAIN

'We regret we are unable to give you the weather. We rely on weather reports from the airport, which is closed because of the weather. Whether we are able to give you the weather tomorrow depends on the weather.'

Arab News, 1979

PERFECTLY UNDERSTOOD, NORMAN

'Thank you for inviting me to participate in "The World's Worst Predictions". It is good of you to ask me but I must decline.'

Norman St John Stevas, 1984

'With the passing of Pope John Paul II the world has lost one of its major figures, leaving a gap which will not easily be filled . . .'

Obituary of the present Pope accidentally printed in the *Nigerian News*, October 1983. Author: Norman St John Stevas

WRITTEN IN HASTE

Letters They Wished They'd Never Sent

Someone, somewhere needs a letter from you . . . but take care how you word it. Putting pen to paper has compromised lovers, convicted criminals and given endless encouragement to the Inland Revenue.

According to GPO regulations no envelope may be more than two feet long, but it takes only a few words inside to make a fool of yourself. A registrar in the North of England lovingly preserves a request from Australia which reads: 'Please forward details of my marriage, the date, the church and the name of the girl I married.'

Some struggle manfully to undo the mishaps of others. 'Dear Sir,' wrote a reader to an American newspaper in 1930, 'I desire to call your attention to a few errors in your obituary notice of myself on Wednesday last. I was born in Washington, not Wheeler, and my retirement from the flour and feed business was not due to ill health, but hard times. The cause of my death was not pneumonia . . .'

And here are one or two more who appeared in black and white and later turned red all over . . .

PLAY IT AGAIN, GEORGE

'I have decided not to play football again, and this time no one will change my mind.'

George Best to Manchester United
Football Club, 1973

A WING AND A PRAYER

'I have been thinking for some time of the advisability of my taking a college course ... I do not think I am specially fitted for success in any commercial pursuit.'

Aviation pioneer Wilbur Wright to his father, Bishop Wright

CONFIDENTLY YOURS

'I hope to write another [novel] fairly soon. It is bound to be a failure, but I know with some clarity what kind of book I want to write.'

George Orwell, to a friend, before embarking on *1984*, *c.* 1948

THE BOVVER WITH A HOVER

'Sorry, such a vehicle is outside our terms of reference ...'

Marconi executive to Christopher Cockerill, turning down his Hovercraft invention

LOVE IS ... LOSING YOUR HEAD

'Praying you also that, if ever before I have done you offence, you will give me that same absolution that you ask, ensuring you that henceforth my heart shall be dedicated to you alone ...'

Henry VIII to Anne Boleyn, 1527. Nine years later she was beheaded

NEEDLED

'You cannot urge too insistently that the objection to vaccination as a quite infamously careless and ignorant method of inoculation should become more obvious than ever.'

George Bernard Shaw, 1906, to Charles Gare, of the Anti-Vaccination League

THE MAN WHO ALMOST HAD HIS WHISKERS CREMATED

'The Act . . . was forced through Parliament in this form by Mr Aneurin Bevan. It gives him more absolute authority than any man in peace has had since Cromwell. He can, on plea of National Health, prohibit beards, or make cremation compulsory, and is answerable to nobody but Parliament.'

Anonymous letter to the *British Medical Journal*, 1946, about the National Health Act

'How come it only applies to Conservatives?'

THE WIDE BLUE YONDER

Kitty Hawk to the Cosmos

Somewhere up there, it has been calculated that there are a hundred thousand billion stars. So far we are a long way from reaching even one of them, but if some 'experts' had been heeded we'd still have our feet firmly on the ground.

Early flight was a traumatic experience. Pioneer balloonist Pierre Blanchard only made the first crossing of the Channel by the seat of his pants. He threw them overboard to gain height as his bulbous craft skimmed the waves. Then, in a last effort to avert disaster he emptied his bladder after them – to his great relief, the balloon slowly inched skyward again.

But for each intrepid pioneer there were scores of the 'it'll never fly' brigade ready to pour scorn on their efforts. Thank heavens, then, for those who doggedly followed their intuition – even if it did occasionally take them where they did not precisely intend going.

Take 'Wrong Way' Corrigan, the 1930s aviator who rumbled down a New York runway heading into the dusk for California. Next morning, to his surprise, he touched down in Ireland. They laughed, of course, but at least he had expanded his horizons. With the right technology, he might even have been the first man in orbit, en route to the office, of course.

BLAST! – 1

'Man will never set his foot on the moon . . .'

> Sir Harold Spencer Jones, *Astronomer Royal*, 1957

GETTING IN A FLAP

'I think it most unlikely that aeronautics will ever be able to exercise a decisive influence on travel. Man is not an albatross . . .'

> H. G. Wells, 1901

CONCORDE, 2 – BOEING, 3

'Aerial transport of goods will never be able to compete with land transport. Flying will be restricted to military and sporting use. Although military purposes seem rather doubtful – sporting uses, on the contrary, are fairly certain.'

> *Engineering News*, 1908

BLAST! – 2

'No rocket will reach the moon save by a miraculous discovery of an explosive far more energetic than any known.'

> Nikola Tesla, inventor, 1928

THANKS FOR THE SUPPORT, POP

'They'll never do it. It is only given to God and angels to fly.'

> Bishop Wright, father of Orville and Wilbur, before the first-ever powered flight at Kitty Hawke, 1903

WAY OUT

'They are already circling, but only in the heads of dreamers . . .'

Aeronautics Journal, 1949. Article on
artificial satellites

LISTEN, SUNSHINE . . .

'To maintain that the sun is immovable is an absurd proposition, false in philosophy, heretical in religion and contrary to the testament of scripture.'

Council of Seven Cardinals condemning
Galileo, 1633

THE FLYING TRAFFIC JAM

'I am convinced that within a few years every household will have one or several flying machines.'

Helicopter pioneer, Hermann
Ganswindt, 1891

MINOR TURBULENCE

'We anticipate a dull and boring flight . . .'

NASA director William Schneider on the
Skylab 3 mission, 1973. Astronauts nearly
had to be rescued when a gas leak
triggered high cabin temperatures. The
crew made emergency repairs and went on
to land upside down in the sea

BELIEVE ME . . .

'The R101 is as safe as a house . . .'

Lord Thomson, secretary of state for air,
1930, as he embarked on the fated maiden
flight of Britain's greatest airship

UP, UP AND AWAY

'Aerial journeys by two persons of different sex are immoral – the pressure of air could be dangerous to the delicate organs of a young girl.'

Vossische Zeitung, 1798

TELL IT TO THE BIRDS

'No possible combination of known substances, known form of machinery and known form of force can be united in a practical machine by which we will fly long distances through the air.'

Dr Simon Newcombe, US scientist, 1900

THROUGH A TELESCOPE DARKLY

'The future of interplanetry travel is utter bilge.'

Professor Richard Woolley, *Astronomer Royal*, 1956

HEAVY ARGUMENT

'The gas turbine is unsuitable as a means of propulsion for aircraft, by reason of its extreme weight.'

US Navy Committee, 1937

NOT EVEN WITH ROLLS-ROYCE ENGINES

'I do not think that a flight across the Atlantic will be made in our lifetime. Moreover, owing to the lightness of the air, in which the aeroplane has to operate, I do not think it will ever be used to carry either goods, or a large number of passengers.'

The Hon. Charles Stewart Rolls, motor
car engineer, *c.* 1909

JUST 41 ACTUALLY

'Landing and moving around the moon offers so many serious problems for human beings that it may take science another 200 years to lick them.'

Science Digest, 1948

ORDER, ORDER

The Wonderful World of Politics

'Being President', according to satirist David Frye, 'is never having to say you're sorry.' Especially when you're running for election, he might have added.

Voting time is probably the only occasion when we all live in the Promised Land, and after all that hard campaigning it is little wonder that politicians suffer from tiredness and emotion.

Lord Brougham, who died in 1868, needed such constant refreshment that he once slid to his knees during a speech. He tried unsuccessfully to get up, then entreated his fellow peers to pass the Bill – literally from the floor of the House.

Ward Hunt, a former chancellor, rose to deliver a budget speech and found to his horror that the dispatch box was missing. He turned pale and almost collapsed as a frantic search got under way. Half an hour later the papers were found – back on his desk at the Treasury.

The modern answer, of course, would be to file everything on tape. As Richard Nixon once said: 'I may be bothered about the taping equipment, but I'm damn glad we have it.'

NUTS ...

'If we just keep up the pressure, those little guys will crack . . .'

US General Earle Wheeler on the Viet Cong, 1970

MAGGIE MAY

'I do not think there will be a woman prime minister in my lifetime.'

Education minister, Margaret Thatcher
on BBC-TV's 'Blue Peter', 1973

SINGA-LONGA-JOE

'Gaiety is the most outstanding feature of life in the Soviet Union.'

Josef Stalin, 1933

' The punchline to the last joke will be incorporated in the next five-year plan.'

TRIGGER HAPPY

'The United States has much to offer the Third World War . . .'

Ronald Reagan, 1975. During his
presidential campaign he made the gaffe
no fewer than nine times in one speech

THE MAN WE'D ALL LIKE TO MEET

'In all likelihood, world inflation is over.'
World Monetry Fund spokesman, 1959

ORANGE JUICE

'I have never made an inflammatory statement in my life.'
Rev. Ian Paisley, 1969

POINTED REMARK

'We rule by love – not by the bayonet.'
Josef Goebbels, 1936

POLITICAL MUSCLE

'I'll count to five and then I'll pull it . . .'
Prime Minister James Callaghan, 1978,
unveiling a plaque at the Anglo-Austrian
Society. Five seconds later he jerked the
cord – and wrenched the entire plaque
from the wall

OIL BE DAMNED

'The possession of this Russian territory can give us
neither honor, wealth, or power, but will always be a
source of weakness and expense, without any adequate
return.'

US Congressman Orange Ferriss, 1868,
on the purchase of Alaska

OOPS!

'This is a discredited president.'

> Richard Nixon, 1974, in a nationwide TV broadcast at the height of Watergate. He intended to say: 'This is a discredited precedent.' But somehow the truth will always out

'Thank you, Governor Evidence.'

> Richard Nixon, 1974, to Washington Governor Dan Evans

'Whenever any mother or father talks to his child, I hope he can look at the man in the White House and, whatever he may think of his politics, he will say: "Well, there is a man who maintains the kind of standards personally I would want my child to follow!"'

> Richard Nixon, 1973

WHICH YEAR, HE ISN'T SAYING

'I give Castro a year, no longer.'

> Deposed President Fulgencio Batista, 1959

EAT, DRINK AND BE MERRY

'Up until recent times the production of food has been the prime struggle of man. That war is won.'

> Winston Churchill, 1932, in *Fifty Years Hence*

HE KNEW MY FATHER . . .

'I'm sorry he is going, but some day he will be prime minister again.'

King George V on receiving Lloyd
George's resignation, 1922

FANTASY ISLAND

'Iran is an island of stability in one of the more troubled areas of the world . . .'

President Jimmy Carter, 1977

TRUTH OR CONSEQUENCES

'Let us begin by committing ourselves to the truth – to see it like it is, and tell it like it is – to find the truth, and to live the truth.'

Richard Nixon launching his presidential
campaign, 1968

HE CAME, HE SAW, HE CONQUERED

'I am proud to be called the conqueror of the British Empire . . .'

Idi Amin, February 1978

NEW FIREFIGHTING TECHNIQUES

'Pish! A woman might piss it out!'

Lord Mayor of London, 1666, on being
told of the Pudding Lane blaze which
started the fire of London

IN THE DOLEDRUMS

'The government's policies are designed to bring unemployment down.'

> Sir Geoffrey Howe, 1980, before
> unemployment rose to 1½ million

'We are beginning to win through ... There are now clear signs that the worst of the recession is over.'

> Prime Minister Margaret Thatcher, 1981,
> before unemployment rose to 2½ million

NEVER BELIEVE AN ACTOR

'Actors are citizens and should exert those rights by speaking their minds, but the actor's first duty is to his profession. Hence you may rest assured that I will never run for anything but head man in my own household.'

> Ronald Reagan, in an interview with the
> *Hollywood Reporter*, 1955

NICE ONE, DICK

'There can be no whitewash at the White House.'

> Richard Nixon, March 1973

ARFUR MINUTE ...

'As far as I'm concerned I recognize that my credibility with this union is completely intact.'

> Miners' leader Arthur Scargill, 1983

SPRINGTIME FOR HITLER

'We are winning international respect.'

Adolf Hitler, 1934

GOING ... GOING ...

'I have no intention of resigning. The president is not going to leave the White House until January 20th, 1977.'

Richard Nixon, August 1974. A week later
he resigned

EBONY AND IVORY

'Rhodesia is a model for the rest of the world as far as race relations are concerned. I know of no happier country.'

Ian Smith, 1967

NICE ONE, SHIRL

'I am not interested in a third party. I do not believe it has any future.'

Shirley Williams, 1980

HOOVERING UP THE MESS

'We in America today are nearer to final triumph over poverty than ever before in the history of the land.'

President Herbert Hoover, 1928, the year
before the Great American Depression

ALL CHANGE

'There are going to be no dramatic changes in Rhodesia.'

Ian Smith, 1975. Independence came just
five years later

WELL, ONE OR THE OTHER ...

'I hope that Spiro Agnew will be completely exonerated and found guilty of the charges against him.'

John Connally, defending his friend Spiro
Agnew, 1973

PROBLEMS, PROBLEMS

'Our only problem at the moment is the problem of success.'

Prime Minister Edward Heath, 1973, the
'winter of discontent'. A few months later
he was out of office

IF THE HALO FITS ...

'The Ayatollah Khomeini will one day be viewed as some kind of saint . . .'

US ambassador to the UN, Andrew Young, 1978

WHO FIXED JIM?

'It's the survival of the fittest, my friend.'

Teamsters Union leader Jimmie Hoffa, one month before he disappeared in 1975

' I've told you before. One stiff to two parts concrete! '

A BLACK FUTURE

'We shall reach the helm within five years.'

Sir Oswald Mosley, fascist, 1938

GIVE ME TIME TO MULLAH IT OVER

'No one can overthrow me . . .'

The Shah of Iran, 1978

'I should like to take a vacation . . .'

The Shah of Iran, 1979

PRIVATE AFFAIRS

'There are things that one passionately wants to keep private. Things that are no one's business. What isn't realized is how professionally I don't expose what I don't want to.'

Jeremy Thorpe, 1974, in Susan Barnes'
Behind the Image

ONE FOR THE ROAD

'Don't drink and drive.'

Campaign devised by Transport Minister
Ernest Marples. In 1974 he was arrested
on a drink/drive charge

BUT HE SURE CAN FLY

'The Shah cannot, will not, and is legally incapable of abdicating.'

Iranian diplomat Ardeshir Zahedi, 1979

NEVER BELIEVE A POLITICIAN

'I think I feel a little better.'

Final words of Viscount Palmerston, 1865

BUT CAN HE CHEW GUM AND WALK AT THE SAME TIME?

'I believe President Nixon – like Abraham Lincoln – is a man uniquely suited to serve our nation in a time of crisis.'

Gerald Ford, 1969

ROTTEN APPLE

'The police are fully able to meet and compete with the criminals.'

Major John Hylan of New York City, 1922

DROPPED BALLS

A Selection of Good Sports

The history of sport is brimming with over-confident participants who opened their mouths, only to find a fist or foot thrust in them.

Unfortunately in some of the best incidents the victims found themselves totally lost for words. Like boxer Joe MacDonald who promised to annihilate his opponent in Niagara Falls, Ontario, in 1949. When he climbed into the ring and peeled off his dressing gown, he realized he had forgotten to put on his shorts.

Or ecstatic striker Rafael Rafaelos who scored his first goal for Bogota and, overcome, grabbed the referee who had awarded the penalty and planted a kiss on his cheek. The ref replied by flooring him with a left hook.

Others try very hard to say something suitable, but fail miserably. The starter at Goodwood in 1830, for instance, was a white-haired gentleman of great age who caused havoc with his uncontrollable stammer. Horses wheeled and plunged as jockeys strained to make out whether he was trying to say 'Go' or 'No' – the order to hold back.

The more articulate – or not, as the case may invariably be – have a high rate of egg on the face when making predictions. Brian Clough never quite lived up to his own advice: 'Say nowt, win it, then talk your head off.' But who minds? As American baseball player Reggie Jackson once said: 'Fans don't boo nobodies . . .'

A MATCHLESS PERFORMANCE

'I make bold to say that I don't believe that in the future history of the world any such feat will be performed by anybody else.'

> The mayor of Dover, 1875, greeting
> Captain Webb, the first man to swim the
> English Channel. Dover District Council
> have since given up counting the hundreds
> of successful Channel-swim attempts

LIVER-WHO?

'Listen, Liverpool aren't a good team – they haven't even got a good coach.'

> John Bond, manager of Norwich FC,
> 1977. Hours later Liverpool beat
> Norwich 6–0

STUNG BY A BEE

'The man who will whip me will be fast, strong – and hasn't been born yet.'

> Muhammed Ali before meeting defeat at
> the hands of Joe Frazier, 1971

NOT SO FRIENDLY

'We have nothing against sport – just the opposite, in fact . . .'

> Commander of German occupying forces
> in Kiev, 1942. Kiev then beat the German
> army 6–0 in a 'friendly' football match and
> were led away by a firing squad

GOLD MEDAL FOR OVERSPENDING

'The Olympic Games can no more have a deficit than a man can have a baby.'

> Mayor Jean Drapeau of Montreal, before the 1976 Olympics, which cost the city $1 billion

HE WALKS . . . HE TALKS . . .

'We feel that Mark Spitz will have a major motion picture career – I can see him playing the lead man in anything he does.'

> Norman Brokaw, Hollywood agent, 1972

. . . AND WHAT A VOICE

'All we've got to do is put a ukelele in his hands and the girls will scream.'

> Agent Sherm Chavoor, 1972, on the plans for Mark Spitz starting a singing career

DID HE EVER MAKE FLEET STREET?

'He will never hold down a first-team place in top-class soccer.'

> Local sports columnist in Stoke on Trent
> on the debut of Sir Stanley Matthews, 1932

NEW BALLS, PLEASE

'She's a great player – for a girl. But no woman can beat a man who knows what he's doing. I'm not only interested in glory for my sex – I want to see women's lib back twenty years, to get women back in the home where they belong.'

> Tennis star Bobby Riggs, 1973, before
> playing Billy Jean King. She thrashed him
> in three straight sets, 6–4, 6–3, 6–3

DROPPED BALL

Frail-looking Aussie Brian Bevan asked Leeds RL club to give him a trial in 1945. The manager told him:
'It would be criminal to send you out with the big boys. The game's too rough for you, son.'

> Bevan's world scoring record of 796 tries
> has never been broken

FIST IN MOUTH

'I'm gonna beat up on him so bad, it'll be a total mismatch.'

> Muhammed Ali before being beaten by
> Larry Holmes, 1979

OVER THE TOP

'People talk about the generation gap, the missile gap, the education gap. I suddenly saw that the real gap was right out there in the heart of the Golden West. And I knew I could bridge the bastard!'

> Evil Knievil, US motorcycle stunt-man, 1974, before his unsuccessful attempt to jump the Grand Canyon

NICE TRY

'I want a team capable of playing positive attacking rugby, and that's why this team has been chosen.'

> Lions coach Jim Telfer before the 1983 New Zealand tour, in which they lost all four Tests

SILVER LINING

'The Olympic movement appears as a ray of sunshine through clouds of racial animosity, religious bigotry and political chicanery.'

> Avery Brundage, president of the International Olympic Committee, 1972, year of the Munich Olympics

AND THOSE WHO HAVE GROVELLING THRUST UPON THEM

'These West Indians – when they're on top, they're magnificent, but when they're down they grovel.'

> England cricket captain Tony Greig, 1976, before England's spectacular defeat by West Indies

FOR CRUYFF'S SAKE, JOHANN!

'Football doesn't pay much.'

Johann Cruyff, 1973

SONNY SIDE UP

'My only worry about Cassius Clay is whether they can get a doctor who can get my glove out of his mouth without cutting my wrist.'

Sonny Liston, 1963

LIFE OF BRIAN

'I'm delighted to be going to Leeds as manager – I don't foresee any problems.'

Soccer manager, Brian Clough, 1974. Six months later he quit

WAR CRIES

The Awesome Might of the Military Mind

It is significant that the phrase 'over the top' should have originated in trench warfare. War, by definition, usually is.

'Anyone may begin a war at his pleasure ...' Machiavelli declared. And a cursory glance at history proves him right: tennis balls, an ear, postage stamps, Easter eggs and a soccer result have triggered international conflict over the years.

He wisely added that wars, however, are rather more difficult to bring to an end. Liechtenstein, for instance, is still technically fighting Prussia because no one bothered to get round to declaring peace.

The general progress of the military mind is uninspiring. From Nelson's 'I see no ships', as he fiddled with the telescope against his blind eye, to the telexed Grenada invasion warnings the Foreign Office had to collect from a London plastics factory – we haven't come very far.

'He finds the subject interesting, but makes little headway,' as my old housemaster would have put it. After reading the predictions which follow, you would be forgiven for thinking that we would all be safer sticking to peace.

WHAT'S THAT DRONING OUTSIDE, JOE?

'No enemy planes will fly over Reich territory.'
> Joseph Goebbels, Nazi minister for
> Propaganda and Public Enlightenment,
> twenty-four hours before the first
> Wellingtons bombed Germany

EVEN IF WE ARE BEATEN

'Whatever happens in Vietnam, I can conceive of nothing except military victory.'
> Lyndon B. Johnson, 1967

HORN OF PLENTY

'Hold your horses, boys. There's plenty down here for us all . . .'
> Attributed to General Custer, 1876, as he
> approached Little Big Horn

OUT FOR A DUCK

'They couldn't hit an elephant at this dist—'
> Last words of Union General John
> Sedgwick struck down by a cannonball in
> the American Civil War

WHAT'S THAT RUMBLING OUTSIDE?

'To this city of Paris, where the German flag shall fly for a thousand years.'
> German Field Marshall Hugo Sperrie,
> proposing a toast two days before the
> liberation of Paris

NO NUKES

'A 3000-mile high-angle rocket shot from one continent to another, carrying an atomic bomb – I say technically, I don't think anyone in the world knows how to do such a thing. I think we can leave that out of our thinking. I wish the American public would leave that out of their thinking.'

Defence engineer, Dr Vannevar Bush, in a
report to a Senate committee, 1945

DRY ROT

'When this message is discovered 1000 years from now, the whole earth will be glorifying the doctrines of our beloved Chancellor Adolf Hitler who will live and grow like this oak.'

Message buried in oak tree, Herford,
Westphalia, 1939. In 1945 the tree was
chopped down

PLAIN SAILING

'The day of the battleship has not passed, and it is highly unlikely that an airplane, or fleet of them, could ever successfully sink a fleet of navy vessels under battle conditions.'

Franklin D. Roosevelt, US assistant
secretary of the navy, 1922

BACK TO THE DRAWING BOARD

'In the twentieth century war will be dead, the scaffold will be dead, animosity will be dead, but man will live.'

Victor Hugo, 1842

'Great news! they've abolished quartering.'

WASTE PAPER

'I believe it is peace for our time.'
Prime Minister, Neville Chamberlain
after the Munich Agreement, September 1938

WE'RE RIDING ALONG ON THE CREST OF A WAVE . . .

'I do not myself think that any civilized nation will torpedo unarmed and defenceless merchant ships.'
Admiral Penrose Fitzgerald, 1914. In May
1915 the Germans torpedoed the
Lusitania

WRONG AGAIN

'I have a hunch that the war will be over before the spring. It won't be by defeat in the field, but by German realization that they can't win.'
Prime Minister Neville Chamberlain,
1939

DAMN

'No enemy bomber is capable of reaching the Ruhr . . .'
Reichsmarshall Hermann Goering, 1939

EVERYBODY CONGA

'The war in Vietnam is going well and will succeed.'
Robert McNamara, US Secretary of
Defence, 1963

THINK TANK

'The idea that cavalry will be replaced by these iron coaches is absurd.'

Unknown general to Field Marshall Haig
inspecting the first tanks, 1916

A FLASH IN THE PAN

'Atomic energy might be as good as our present-day explosives, but it is unlikely to produce anything very much more dangerous.'

Winston Churchill, 1939

STRICTLY FOR THE WETS

'I must confess that my imagination refuses to see any sort of submarine doing anything but suffocating its crew and floundering at sea.'

H. G. Wells, 1901

PACK UP YOUR TROUBLES

'Mothers and fathers . . . I have said this before, but I shall say it again and again: your boys are not going to be sent into any foreign wars.'

President Franklin Roosevelt, 1940

FISHY BUSINESS

'A damned silly trifling novelty that will never catch on . . .'

Seventeenth-century Admiralty report on
an early form of submarine

SOME YOU WIN . . .

The Things They Say

Foot in mouth disease shows little sign of diminishing. Few aspects of life have been left untouched, including religion.

A 1935 Church of England commission declared that clergywomen would not be a good idea. Male worshippers, they concluded, would not be able to listen to a sermon 'without becoming unduly conscious of her sex'.

Even death holds no respite. It was Viscount Templewood who formed the opinion in 1951 that 'Executions are so much a part of British history that it is almost impossible for many excellent people to think of the future without them.' I can fortunately think of better ways of spending an afternoon.

When it comes to business, however, there are those who know exactly what they're about. Like the American garden centre which advertises: 'If your miracle shade tree doesn't grow up to roof high in the first season, if it doesn't soar higher than even the magnificent winged elm, taller than even the stately mountain ash, wider than even the most majestic poplar . . . then simply post it back to us and your money will be refunded – no questions asked.'

DON'T CALL US . . .

'His brain is addled . . .'
Teacher's report expelling Thomas
Edison from school, *c.* 1860

TOASTED

'We wish you long life and happiness with Lady Jane . . .'
Industrialist Peter Balfour toasting Prince
Charles on his engagement to Lady Diana
in 1981

BITING THE BULLET

'The bullet hasn't been made that can kill me.'
Jack 'Legs' Diamond, Chicago gangster
gunned down in 1931

GREAT STRIDES HAVE BEEN MADE

'In no circumstances shall a preacher who
wears trousers ever be allowed to
occupy a pulpit.'
Trust deed of a Kent
Nonconformist chapel, 1820

A CROWN JEWEL

'There is no romance, and no grounds for these rumours of a romance . . .'

Princess Anne, shortly before her
engagement to Mark Phillips, 1973

POLE VAULT

'It is too early for a Polish pope.'

Cardinal Karol Wojtyla, 14th October
1978. On 16th October he became Pope
John Paul II

HAVE YOU HUGGED YOUR TICKET COLLECTOR TODAY?

'We have to make it an obsession to cherish our customers and make them love us.'

Bob Reid, chairman of British Rail, 1984

'The price includes rail fare and two nights in a top London hotel with the porter of your choice.'

SOMETHING TO CHEW OVER

'Alfred Packer exemplifies the spirit and fare that this Agriculture Department cafeteria will provide . . .'

> US agriculture secretary Robert Bergland, opening the Alfred Packer Memorial Dining Facility in 1977. The commemorative plaque was later removed on discovering that Packer, a nineteenth-century Colorado pioneer, was convicted of murdering and eating five prospectors in 1874

NIL DESPERANDUM

'I'm too old for marriage.'

> Angus Ogilvy, 1962. A year later he was married to Princess Alexandra

LOW PROFILE

'Stay out of sight and you stay out of trouble.'

> President John F. Kennedy

RELATIVELY DULL

'He will never amount to anything.'
Albert Einstein's Munich High School report

BIRD BRAIN

'Keep back – it will claw your eyes out . . .'
Runcorn chartered surveyor holding
police at bay with his pet falcon, 1982. A
violent struggle ensued when the bird
turned on its owner. Officers had to
rescue him by smothering it with a blanket

TINKER TAYLOR

'I try to keep a healthy body, that's all there is to it.'
Elizabeth Taylor, 1966

MUM'S THE WORD

'I would actually decry the notion that there is a recession.'
Mark Thatcher, 1984

THE LAST DROP

'Of course the water's safe to drink . . .'
Novelist Arnold Bennett, Paris, 1931,
before draining a glass from which he
caught typhoid and died

... LONG TO REIGN OVER US

'I have no intention of resigning my title. Is that understood?'

> Miss World Marjorie Wallace, 1973.
> Three days later she resigned

SWASHBUCKLED

'I've never felt better.'
Last words of Douglas Fairbanks Snr, 1939

BLOW ME

'Hurricane Gloria will not strike Taiwan.'

> Formosa Weather Bureau, 1964. It did,
> wrecking £8 million worth of property

APPLE BUTTER DOESN'T HIT THE FAN

'This goddamn mountain won't blow. Those scientists don't know shit from apple butter . . .'

> Harry Truman, resident of Mount St
> Helen, Washington, 1980. Days later the
> volcano blew its top – and Harry with it

SHIVER ME TIMBERS

'This is an earthquake – there is no cause for alarm . . .'

> William James, brother of novelist Henry
> James, in the San Francisco earthquake,
> 1906; 450 people were killed and damage
> was estimated at £147 million

HE MUST HAVE CHANGED HIS MIND

'The world will end in a great flood on February 20th, 1524.'

Johannes Stoeftler, astrologer, University
of Tubingen, January 1524

BAFFLING BOFFINS

The Misappliance of Science

Back in the 1800s, Dr Dionysius Lardner, of University College, London, had reservations about the age of the train. Railway travel over 10 m.p.h., he declared with expert conviction, was impossible 'because passengers, unable to breathe, would die of asphyxia'. He obviously hadn't met Jimmy Savile.

Scientists have a knack of putting their foot in it. In 1962 NASA lost £9 million when Mariner I disappeared into the blue because a hyphen was missed out of the formula to plot its course.

Even the great have their moments. Cambridge geneticist J. B. S. Haldane said half a century ago: 'I do not believe in the possibility of anything much worse than mustard gas being produced.'

Perhaps they should all take a leaf from Einstein's book. When he looked back on his achievements he said: 'If only I had known, I would have been a locksmith.'

YOU CAN ALL GO HOME NOW ...

'Physics is a branch of knowledge which is stable and very largely exhausted. It is really hardly worth studying any longer.'

Physicist Philipp von Jolly, 1875

THE PAIN THRESHOLD

'Knife and pain are two words in surgery that must forever be associated in the consciousness of the patient. To this compulsory combination we shall have to adjust ourselves.'

Surgeon Dr Alfred Velpeau, 1839, seven years before the introduction of general anaesthetic

SO THAT'S WHY WE CAN'T GET THE WASHING MACHINE MENDED

'By 1970 all backbreaking work will be done by machine power, and I mean all. Men will only work six hours a day, four days a week.'

> Professor William Ogburn, American
> sociologist, 1943

THAT'S A RELIEF

'The power of tobacco to sustain the system, to keep up nutrition, to maintain and increase the weight, to brace against severe exertion, and to replace ordinary food, is a matter of daily and hourly demonstration.'

> George Black in *The Doctor at Home*, 1898

I COULD SEE RIGHT THROUGH THEM

'X-rays will prove to be a hoax.'

> Lord Kelvin, president of the Royal
> Society, 1893

ALTERNATIVELY SPEAKING

'There is no plea which will justify the use of high-tension and alternating currents, either in a scientific or a commercial sense. They are employed solely to reduce investment in copper wire and real estate.'

> Thomas Edison, 1889, the year before AC
> was introduced in America

A DROP OF MOONSHINE

'Anyone who looks for a source of power in the transformation of the atom is talking moonshine.'

Ernest Rutherford, 1923

GOD WAS NOT AN EARLY RISER

'Heaven and earth were created in the same instant on October 23rd, 4004 BC, at nine o'clock in the morning.'

Dr John Lightfoot, Vice-Chancellor, Cambridge University, 1858. In 1859 Darwin's *Origin of the Species* was published

EMPTY NOTION

'A vacuum is totally impossible . . .'

Philosopher scientist, René Descartes, 1630

A CUTTING REMARK

'There cannot always be fresh fields of conquest by the knife; there must be portions of the human frame that will ever remain sacred from its intrusions, at least in the surgeon's hands . . . The abdomen, the chest, and the brain will forever be shut from the intrusion of the wise and humane surgeon.'

Sir John Erichsen, surgeon, 1873

POWER ON TAP

'There is no likelihood that man can ever tap the power of the atom.'

Nobel prizewinner Robert Milliken, 1923

MOONSTRUCK

'To hope for an early success is highly optimistic.'
Astronomer Patrick Moore, 1958, on the
possibility of sending a rocket to the dark side
of the moon. It took just fourteen months

AT LAST – AN END TO RADIO ONE

'The population of the earth decreases every day, and if
this continues, in another ten centuries the earth will be
nothing but a desert.'
Charles-Louis Montesquieu, political
philosopher, 1743

THE MIGHTY ATOM

'I can accept the Theory of Relativity as little as I can
accept the existence of atoms and other such dogma.'
Physicist Ernst Mach, 1916

WHO WANTS TO BE A MILLIONAIRE . . .?

Ridiculed Ideas

The junk yards of the world are littered with useless inventions – bright ideas, conceived in optimism and hopeful of making a million.

Whatever happened, for instance, to the Victorian jacket, covered with iron studs and sold as 'an essential piece of luggage for everyone travelling abroad'? The theory was that if a tiger seized the unwary wearer in its jaws, he would prove so indigestible that the disgusted beast would spit him out again.

But for each indigestion-wracked tiger there have been genuine technical breakthroughs which were ignored or ridiculed.

Bell's telephone was panned by London experts as 'the latest American humbug'. And Sir Alexander Parkes, one of the early pioneers of plastic, opened a factory in 1850 to market his remarkable new product – and promptly went bust. 'Sorry, there's no future for it,' retailers said.

On the other hand there are always those for whom the sky's the limit. 'Their meteoric rise to fame', to borrow a phrase from a 'Juke Box Jury' panellist, 'is paralleled only by the swiftness of their descent.' (He was probably referring to the Beatles at the time.)

EVERYTHING'S BLOOMING

'Home movie equipment – it'll be easy.'

> Washing-machine king John Bloom,
> announcing new business directions
> in 1964

'The TV rental business . . . there shouldn't be any problem making money there. And think of the business when colour comes in!'

> Three months later John Bloom's financial
> empire collapsed

WHERE IS HE NOW?

'I think there is a world market for about five computers.'

> Thomas Watson, IBM executive, 1958

THE TRIPEWRITER

'No mere machine can replace a reliable and honest clerk . . .'

> Remington Arms Company, 1898, on
> being offered the rights to manufacture
> the typewriter

YOU CAN'T BEAT A GOOD SCREW

'We are watching with interest all the work on jet engines abroad. But scientific investigation here has shown that this process can in no way compete with the combination of motor and airscrew . . .'

> British under-secretary for defence, 1934

COURTING DISASTER

'It's not going to fail. It's going to be very successful . . .'
                                    John De Lorean, October 1978

DOWN THE TUBES – 1

'Television won't last. It is a flash in the pan.'
                            Radio technologist and pioneer Mary
                                            Somerville, 1948

DOWN THE TUBES – 2

'It is a small manufacturing tolerance error, which will be
very simple to correct . . .'
                            Spokesman for Birmingham engineers
                            Metro-Cammell, who produced a dozen
                            train carriages too wide for the London
                                            Tube in 1984

A TWIST ABOUT NOTHING

'The public will never accept artificial silks. Listers will
stay with the real thing.'
                            Bradford silk mill directors, upon being
                            offered the rights to manufacture rayon
                                            in 1912

A COUPLE OF BRIGHT SPARKS

'It must be considered illusory to think that radio will ever
supercede wire telegraphy.'

                            Professor Ferdinand Braun, 1900

'Radio has no future . . .'
Lord Kelvin, president of the Royal Society, 1904

GETTING HIS LINES CROSSED

'The Americans may have need of the telephone, but we
do not. We have plenty of messenger boys.'
Chief GPO engineer Sir William Preece, 1876

THE MEN WHO ALMOST PASSED GO

'It will take too long to play. The rules are too compli-
cated, and players keep going round and round the board
instead of ending at a final goal.'
Parker Brothers, America's biggest games
manufacturer, rejecting Monopoly, 1934.
A year later they made a U-turn and
bought the rights. It has since been played
by 250 million people

HOW TO GET UP SOMEONE'S NOSE

'I just pray to God that the UK government spend their
North Sea oil revenue intelligently, instead of continuing
to pour money into subsidising businesses that are losers
from day one.'
John De Lorean, 1979

ON YER BIKE

'The ordinary "horseless carriage" is at present a luxury
for the wealthy, and although its price will probably fall in
the future, it will never, of course, come into as common
use as the bicycle.'
The Literary Digest, 1889

IT ISN'T WORTH A LIGHT

'Your cigar-ettes will never become popular.'

Notts cigar makers, E. G. Alton turning
down an investment proposal by John
Player, *c.* 1890

WHAT A GAS

'He wants to light London with gas! A madman – one of those dull ones who are quite in earnest – the most hopeless of all!'

Sir Walter Scott, 1910, on F. A.
Windsor's proposals for London street
lighting. Two years later Scott's home was
gas lit

'They might as well try to light London with a slice from the moon.'

William Wollaston, nineteenth-century chemist

IF GOD HAD INTENDED ...

'They pervert the natural sight, thus making things appear in an unnatural, and therefore false, light.'

The Reverend Crosse,
nineteenth-century vicar of Chew Magna,
on spectacles

DUMMY

'You are imposing on us. Do you imagine we are to be fooled by a ventriloquist?'

Professor Bouillard, French scientist who
seized Edison by the throat at the first
demonstration of the phonograph

HE WAS IN FOR A SHOCK

'With regard to electric light, much has been said for and against it, but I think I may say, without fear of contradiction, that when the Paris Exhibition closes, electric light will close with it, and very little more will be heard of it.'

Professor Erasmus Wilson, 1878, on the first demonstrations of electricity

NOT REVOLUTIONARY

'They will never try to steal the phonograph – it is not of any commercial value.'

Thomas Edison, 1915

OUT OF ORDER

'You could put in this room all the radio telephone apparatus that the country will ever need.'

W. W. Dean, Telephone Company president, 1907

OH, REALLY?

'Everything that can be invented has been invented.'

Report to US President William McKinley from the American Patent Office, 1899

JET LAG

'Very interesting, Whittle my boy, but it will never work.'

Unidentified Cambridge professor of aeronautical engineering, to jet engine inventor Sir Frank Whittle, *c.* 1930

TRAVELLING HOPEFULLY
Land and Sea Travel

The only reason we all aren't clip-clopping up and down the M1 on horseback is ingenuity.

Early transport inventors were imbued with the Right Stuff. When Karl Benz chugged around in the first petrol-driven motor car, there was a splutter of sparks, and it ground to a halt with an electrical short circuit. Mrs Benz solved the problem by whipping off her garter to insulate the wiring.

It is perhaps no coincidence that driving tests became mandatory on April Fool's Day.

Ingenuity at sea is a prerequisite of the job. In 1983 the captain of a £20 million hovercraft stranded in mid-Channel, borrowed a passenger's spanner, effected an engine repair and carried on to France.

Despite advances in technology, however, some of the latest developments in sea power are left high and dry. Four new crack minesweepers, built for the Italian navy, were stranded in the shipyard because a river bridge was too low to allow access to the open sea. Now they didn't have that problem with the *Titanic* . . .

THE HAND OF GOD

'Madam, God himself could not sink this ship . . .'
Crew member of the *Titanic* to a
passenger, 1912

76

A BUNCH OF SQUIRTS

'The public will never consent to be squirted through a drain-pipe.'

> Parliamentary Committee considering
> proposals for the London Underground, 1891

BRIDGE THAT GAP

'No single-span bridge can be built wider than six hundred feet. I know, I built the one at Menai.'

> Engineer Thomas Telford. Nine years
> after his death Brunel built a 900-foot
> span bridge

CHITTY CHITTY CLANG CLANG

'The car is not worth a damn.'

Ernest Breech, vice president of Ford Motors
on being offered the opportunity to
manufacture VW Beetles after World War II

'The Volkswagen does not meet the fundamental technical requirements of a motorcar . . .'

Sir William Rootes turning down a similar
opportunity to produce VWs in Britain

SS HAVANNA

'Do you propose to drive a steam ship with cigar smoke?'

Napoleon Bonaparte to steamship pioneer Robert Fulton

THAT SINKING FEELING

'I cannot imagine any condition which could cause this ship to flounder. I cannot conceive of any vital disaster happening to this vessel. Modern ship building has gone beyond that.'

Captain E. J. Smith, master of the *Titanic*, 1912

TUNNEL VISION

'No person could wish to be shut away from daylight for so long. Passengers would be unable to breathe. Delicate personages might even die from fear of the dark.'

Evidence at Parliamentary Enquiry, 1835,
into plans for a two-mile railway tunnel
between Chippenham and Bath. Twelve
months later work started

NOT SO CHUFFED

When railways chugged into everyday life, critics let off more steam than the hissing locomotives themselves.

The *British Engineering Journal* spluttered in 1825: 'Nothing is more ridiculous than the claim to build a locomotive which will travel at twice the speed of a mail coach.'

'This is the most absurd plan ever invented by a human being . . .'

'Carriages rushing along at 10 m.p.h., drawn by the devil in the shape of a locomotive with Beelzebub himself at the controls. The entire project is absolute madness.'

> Evidence at a Parliamentary enquiry into
> George Stephenson's proposal for a
> railway between Liverpool and Darlington

LAST ORDERS . . .

'We have struck an iceberg, but there is no danger. The ship is unsinkable.'

> Captain's announcement to passengers,
> *Titanic*, 1912

HORSE SENSE

'This cast-iron monster only makes manufactures dearer, and interferes with trade.'

> Society of Berlin Manufacturers'
> comments on the first steam engine of the
> early 1800s

THEY CAN'T PLAY RUGBY EITHER

'We have no coals exported from this port, nor ever shall, as it would be too expensive to bring it down here from the internal part of the country . . .'

Cardiff Collector of Customs, 1782,
reporting to his London superiors

A LOAD OF RUDDER NONSENSE

'If the propeller had the power of propelling a vessel, it would be found altogether useless in practice, because the power being applied in the stern would make it impossible to steer the vessel.'

Sir William Symonds, naval architect, 1837

CREDIBILITY GAP

'Ours has been the first, and will doubtless be the last, party of whites to visit this profitless locality.'

Lieutenant Joseph C. Ives, US Corps of
Topographical Engineers, after surveying
the Grand Canyon, 1861

TRAFFIC PROBLEMS

'There will probably be a mass market for no more than a thousand motor cars in Europe. There is, after all, a limit to the number of chauffeurs who could be found to drive them.'

Spokesman for Daimler-Benz, *c.* 1900